CHI

4|07

FRIENDS
OF ACPL

CORN

Life Cycles

ABDO
Publishing Company

A Buddy Book
by Julie Murray

VISIT US AT
www.abdopublishing.com

Published by ABDO Publishing Company, 4940 Viking Drive, Edina, Minnesota 55435.

Copyright © 2007 by Abdo Consulting Group, Inc. International copyrights reserved in all countries. No part of this book may be reproduced in any form without written permission from the publisher. Buddy Books™ is a trademark and logo of ABDO Publishing Company.

Printed in the United States.

Coordinating Series Editor: Sarah Tieck
Contributing Editor: Michael P. Goecke
Graphic Design: Deb Coldiron
Cover Photograph: Photodisc
Interior Photographs/Illustrations: Brand X Pictures, Corbis, Media Bakery, Photodisc, Photos.com

Library of Congress Cataloging-in-Publication Data

Murray, Julie, 1969–
   Corn / Julie Murray.
      p. cm. — (Life Cycles)
   Includes index.
   ISBN-13: 978-1-59928-705-8
   ISBN-10: 1-59928-705-6
   1. Corn—Life cycles—Juvenile literature. I. Title.

SB191.M2M87 2007
633.1'5—dc22

                                   2006031419

Table Of Contents

What Is A Life Cycle?

Corn plants are living things. The world is made up of many kinds of life. People are alive. So are owls, otters, badgers, and cacti.

Corn plants often grow in large fields.

Every living thing has a life cycle. A life cycle is made up of many changes and processes. During a life cycle, living things are born, they grow, and they reproduce. And eventually, they die. Different living things start life and grow up in unique ways.

What do you know about the life cycle of corn?

All About Corn

Corn is a plant that is grown in fields. It is raised in most areas of the world.

The United States produces the most corn in the world. The state of Iowa grows the most corn in the United States. Actually, Iowa raises more corn than most countries! Only China grows more corn than Iowa.

There are many different types of corn. Some are used as decoration. Others are boiled or popped and covered with caramel to be eaten.

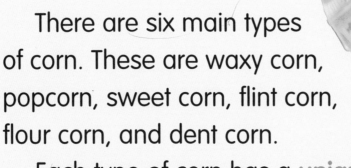

There are six main types of corn. These are waxy corn, popcorn, sweet corn, flint corn, flour corn, and dent corn.

Each type of corn has a **unique** taste, use, and **texture**. Each kind also looks different. Corn comes in many colors, including yellow, white, blue, and red.

People can enjoy corn in several ways. Many people eat sweet corn. And popcorn is a yummy snack.

However, corn has many other uses. Dent, or field, corn is used to feed animals. It is also used to make products such as fuel, plastic, corn oil, and cornstarch.

Cows, chickens, and other farm animals eat field corn.

Corn is ground and used in many everyday products. These include cereals, syrup, paints, and paper goods.

A Corn Plant's Life

A corn plant begins life as a seed. Corn grows best in places with lots of sunlight and warm air. But, scientists have developed corn plants that grow well in cooler weather, too.

The corn plant's growing cycle begins in spring. Farmers plant seeds when the soil is about 50°F (10°C). Once planted, the seeds sprout and cornstalks begin growing.

Over the summer months, the small plants grow bigger and bigger. Soon, an ear of corn appears on the stalk. When the ears are fully grown, it is time to harvest them.

People eat some of the harvested corn. Corn is also used to create important products. Have you ever picked an ear of corn?

An ear of corn on a cornstalk.

Guess What?

…Popcorn is the only type of corn that pops when cooked. The United States grows more of this popular snack food than any other country.

People have been popping popcorn for more than 1,000 years.

…Cornstarch helps make many useful products. These include denim, paper, and the plywood used to make houses.

…The modern corn plant comes from a Mexican grass plant called *teosinte*. *Teosinte* still grows wild in Mexico. However, it does not produce ears of corn.

Starting To Grow

Corn is a crop that is grown in fields. Corn plants produce ears of corn, which are full of kernels. These kernels are the plant's grain, or seeds. Most corn kernels are yellow or white. But, they can be red, blue, or other colors, too.

Corn plants spring up from the ground.

In the past, farmers used their own kernels to start corn plants. But today, most farmers buy their seeds. This helps them grow better crops.

The corn planting **process** starts in the winter months. At that time, farmers plan what types of crops they will plant. They also decide which fields to use. Then, they order seeds.

Kernels of corn are used as seeds for a future generation of corn plants.

When the weather is warm enough, planting begins. Most farmers use machines to help them plant corn crops.

To begin, some farmers plow and clear the remains of last year's crop. Then, they plant new seeds in rows.

Other farmers use a method called "no till." The farmers don't plow or remove crop waste. Instead, they drill through it to plant in the soil below. This helps improve soil quality.

Farmers use machines like this planter to plant several rows of corn at once.

From Seed To Stalk

Once planted, the seeds germinate in the ground. Soon, tiny corn plants come up through the dirt. Sun and rain help the plants grow taller and taller. In some of the early stages, corn plants can grow a couple of inches each day!

After four to six weeks, the corn plants begin forming a tassel and corn silk. This means the plant is able to produce ears of corn. Some stalks grow just one ear. But others may grow more.

The tassel helps with the corn plant's pollinating process.

An ear of corn begins growing when pollen falls from the tassel onto the corn silk. Each strand of silk can accept one grain of pollen. Each strand then makes one kernel of corn. Those kernels grow together to make an ear.

The kernels start out very small. And at the beginning, they are full of liquid sugars. This is called the "milk stage."

Over the warm growing months, the liquid sugars turn into solid starches. So, the corn kernels become more solid as they grow.

Ready To Harvest

In 9 to 11 weeks, the corn plant is fully grown. Farmers look at the plant and kernels for signs that they are ready to be picked. The kernels will be a certain size and dryness.

When the corn is ready, it is time to harvest it. Farmers use large farm machines called combines for this **process**. One combine can pick 8 to 12 rows of corn at once.

A combine separates the ears of corn from the stalk. Then, the combine separates the kernels from the cobs and **husks**. The kernels go into a holding tank. The other parts of the corn are left in the field.

Farmers sell the harvested corn. Trucks take the corn to stores or factories. There, corn is made into products for people to buy and use.

Farmers use combines to harvest corn.

Endings And Beginnings

After harvest, the corn plant dies. But, this is not the end of all corn. Because corn grows kernels and can reproduce, this plant's life continues on.

Every time a farmer plants kernels, it helps create a new generation. This is the beginning of another life cycle.

Can You Guess?

Q: Which U.S. state grows the most corn?
A: Iowa. In fact, it grows more corn than most countries!

Most U.S. corn is grown in an area called the Corn Belt. The Corn Belt includes Iowa, as well as parts of other midwestern states.

Q: Where was corn first grown?
A: Southern Mexico and Central America.

Important Words

generation a group that is living at the same time and is about the same age.

germinate to grow from a seed.

husk the covering that protects an ear of corn.

process a way of doing something.

reproduce to produce offspring, or children.

texture the way something feels when touched.

unique different.

Web Sites

To learn more about corn, visit ABDO Publishing Company on the World Wide Web. Web site links about corn are featured on our Book Links page. These links are routinely monitored and updated to provide the most current information available.

www.abdopublishing.com

Index